# Living *with* PARKINSON'S, DEPRESSION, *and* Childhood Trauma

## A SHORT MEMOIR

## DAWN HOWARD

ISBN 979-8-88644-169-7 (Paperback)
ISBN 979-8-88644-170-3 (Digital)



Covenant Books
11661 Hwy 707
Murrells Inlet, SC 29576
www.covenantbooks.com

Why am I educating people at the beginning of my story?

I am dedicating the first couple of chapters to the education on Parkinson's, anxiety, depression, and child abuse. I feel that by giving a brief summary of each of the things I am dealing with, it may help people understand me better. At the beginning of my diagnosis, I lacked knowledge of these types of illnesses. All that I knew was that Michael J. Fox had Parkinson's and that a few people I had worked with in the past were dealing with mental health issues. My hope is to give people a better understanding of these topics.

# Contents

# Special Thanks

I want to thank the following:

- *My husband*—for always being there, even when I pushed you away. You are my rock, and I appreciate you more than you could ever know. I love you!
- *My daughter*—for just listening to me. You are my whole life, and I can't imagine trying to go through this without you. I love you!
- *My best friend in the world, Ann*—you have been my sounding board and the first person to notice that something was wrong with me. I don't know how I could have dealt with the news had you not been there. You have always been there for me, and I really appreciate it. I love you as a sister!
- *My youngest sister*—you have always been there for me, even when I acted like a fool. You are the strongest person I know. You kicked cancer's butt, and it is your strength that I draw from. I keep telling myself, if my sister can act like a warrior then so can I.
- *To Robbie*—thank you for saving my life that day and giving me a place to stay. Now that you are with God, I know that you know how grateful I am to you.
- *To the singers and songwriters of the songs that I mentioned in this book*—without your music, I wouldn't have pulled through on my darkest days. I sincerely thank you!

# Main Characters

- Me
- Ex-husband—referred to as my husband throughout the story
- Daughter—I only have one child
- Father
- Mother
- Middle sister
- Youngest sister
- Half Brother
- Grandfather
- Best friend, Ann
- Middle-school bully, Jason
- Kindergarten bully, Chad
- Ex-boyfriend, I called Charles
- My ex-boyfriend Robbie

# Introduction

My name is Dawn Howard, and this is my story. At the time of writing this book, I am fifty-one years old, and I have been living with Parkinson's disease for eleven years. I was diagnosed in 2011 at age forty. I have what they call young-onset Parkinson's disease.

Why am I telling you my story?

My answer to this question serves multiple purposes.

1.  It is a way to finally tell my story as seen through my eyes.
2.  I hope that, by telling my story, I may help someone in a similar situation.
3.  To educate people on both Parkinson's, depression, anxiety, and child abuse.
4.  Most importantly, it gives me an outlet to express my feelings, both past and current.
5.  To spread awareness of the foundation I established called Dawn's Hope.

I am not writing and telling my story to portray myself as a victim, nor am I out to hurt or make anyone in this book look bad. The sole purpose of telling my story is for the reasons listed above and for no other reason.

Both of my parents are alive at the time that this book was written and published. I am hoping that people will respect my family's need for privacy. This is my story, not theirs. I do not want any bad to happen to either of my parents. I have long since forgiven my parents, and if you can make it through my book, you will perhaps understand why.

## What is this book about?

This book is my account of my life as seen through my eyes. I will tell my story of being abused by my father, being bullied by classmates, then becoming a middle-aged adult living with Parkinson's disease, depression, and anxiety. I hope that by telling my story, someone in a similar circumstance will realize that if they hold on long enough, they can overcome being a victim and come through it as a survivor who can turn something so ugly into something that only makes them stronger.

## To my readers

Please bear with me as you read my story. I am not an author, a publisher, nor have I ever written a book before. I am not a scientist nor a doctor. Any information quoted or listed in relation to Parkinson's disease, child abuse, and mental illness all come from the sources listed in the reference section of this book. Yes, I copied and pasted a lot of the medical facts in my book. I did so because the authors of what is quoted stated it better than I ever could.

I will do my best not to jump around in telling my story. Keep in mind that I may have to do so in order to explain my reasoning or thoughts behind my current mindset. Also, keep in mind that while writing this, I am disabled and dealing with the many symptoms of my disease, on top of the emotions of having to relive my past. When I get to the part of my story where I was abused, I will not go in great detail for my sake and yours.

I really hope that after reading my story, parents have a serious discussion about the topics I discuss in my book. Don't assume that your child knows right from wrong. Make it clear to your children that they can come to you if something happens to them that makes them feel uncomfortable or sad. Children that are be bullied in school rarely tell their parents about it. A case in point is my daughter. She was bullied in school and never told me about it. I had to hear it from her high school principal. I was lucky because had I not been told, there is no telling what the outcome could have been. Due to advances in technology, bullying has gotten worse because the bullies are now hiding behind a computer screen and don't have to come face to face with their victims. Bullying has led children to believe that they are worthless and the only way out is to kill themselves. Parents who have lost a child to suicide are left confused and wondering how they could have missed the signs. More on this topic will follow in a later chapter.

## Worth noting

Twenty percent of the proceeds from this book will be split equally between the Michael J. Fox Foundation and the Parkinson's Foundation, and 20 percent will go to my foundation, "Dawn's Hope Inc." More on this topic can be found in the last chapter.

# CHAPTER 1

# Parkinson's Disease

## What is Parkinson's?

"Parkinson's disease is a progressive nervous system disorder that affects movement" (https://www.mayoclinic.org/diseases-conditions/parkinsons-disease/).

## What is a progressive disease?

"A progressive *disorder is a disease* or health condition that gets worse over time, resulting in a general decline in health or function" (www.verywellhealth.com).

## History

Parkinson's disease is mentioned in the Bible and as far back as 1000 BC. James Parkinson referred to it as the shaking palsy. It got this name because one of the most common symptoms is shaking tremors.

Shaking Palsy was later changed to Parkinson's disease in 1817, when Jean-Martin Charcot suggested the use of the term 'Parkinson's disease' rejecting the earlier designation of paralysis agitans or shaking palsy.

Charcot recognized that Parkinson's disease patients are not markedly weak and do not necessarily have tremors.

The disease was named after James Parkinson who first medically described Parkinson's as a neurological syndrome.

It was Charcot who separated Parkinson's disease from Multiple Sclerosis and other disorders. (www.ncbi.nlm.nih.gov)

*Symptoms*

A list, along with a brief description of each, can be found by going to mayoclinic.org, and they can also be found on the multiple websites that I have listed in the Reference section. Please note that this is only a summary of the more prominent symptoms.

- Tremor
- Slowness of movement
- Rigid muscles
- Impaired posture and/or balance
- Loss of automatic movements
- Loss of smell
- Speech and writing changes
- Pain
- Fatigue
- Blood pressure issues
- Sexual issues
- Vision issues—dry eyes, double vision
- Masked face

- Depression
- Anxiety
- Cognitive issues
- Swallowing, chewing, eating issues
- Sleep problems
- Bladder and constipation issues
- Restless legs, constant movements, can't keep still
- Vivid dreams

## Causes

In Parkinson's disease, certain nerve cells (neurons) in the brain gradually break down or die. Many of the symptoms are due to a loss of neurons that produce a chemical messenger in your brain called dopamine. When dopamine levels decrease, it causes abnormal brain activity, leading to impaired movement and other symptoms of Parkinson's disease. (www.mayoclinic.org)

## Dopamine

Dopamine is a neurotransmitter. Responsible for transmitting signals between the nerve cells of the brain, dopamine is often called a chemical messenger. It plays a significant role in the body and has a direct impact on our central nervous system. Dopamine affects everything from the way we think and move to the way we remember and behave.

Like the neurotransmitter *serotonin*, which helps regulate mood, dopamine is involved in many psychological illnesses. Abnormally functioning dopamine receptors play a role in some health and mental health disorders. (verywellmind.com)

To date, there isn't a known cause for Parkinson's disease. I personally believe I contracted the disease because of my father's exposure to Agent Orange during the Vietnam War. My uncle, who served in Vietnam and was also exposed to Agent Orange, contracted and died of Parkinson's.

The more I research Vietnam vets and their children, the more and more I am finding that many of them have progressive or life-altering diseases. You have probably seen the commercials showing that if you have been exposed to or used this herbicide and have Parkinson's disease, you may be compensated. You can bet your butt that the government will never admit that Agent Orange has caused damage, not only to those exposed to this chemical but to their children and grandchildren alike. If more studies would be done on this, I bet they would find the link. I also imagine that, if research is done, they will discover that this chemical will have changed the genetic makeup of future generations. We are only at the beginning of discovering the ramifications of the use of this chemical. But this is for another book and not one that I will be writing.

Agent Orange was a powerful herbicide used by U.S. military forces during the Vietnam War to eliminate forest cover and crops for North Vietnamese and Viet Cong troops. The U.S. program, codenamed Operation Ranch Hand, sprayed more than 20 million gallons of various herbicides over Vietnam, Cambodia and Laos from 1961 to 1971. Agent Orange, which contained the deadly chemical dioxin, was the most commonly used herbicide. It was later proven to cause serious health issues—including cancer, birth defects, rashes and severe psychological and neurological problems—among the Vietnamese people as well as among returning U.S. servicemen and their families. (www.history.com/topics/vietnam-war/agent-orange)

*Risk factors for Parkinson's disease include:*

- *Age.* Young adults rarely experience Parkinson's disease. It ordinarily begins in middle or late life, and the risk increases with age. People usually develop the disease around age sixty or older.
- *Heredity.* Having a close relative with Parkinson's disease increases the chances that you'll develop the disease. However, your risks are still small unless you have many relatives in your family with Parkinson's disease.
- *Sex.* Men are more likely to develop Parkinson's disease than are women.
- *Exposure to toxins.* Ongoing exposure to herbicides and pesticides may slightly increase your risk of Parkinson's disease.

Paragraph above is quoted from the following source: https://www.mayoclinic.org/diseases-conditions/parkinsons-disease/.

*Current treatments (www.mayoclinic.org)*

- *Medications* (carbidopa-levodopa pills—inhaled, infusion), *dopamine agonists* (Mirapex, Requip), *MAO-B inhibitors* (Azilect, Xadago), *catechol-O-methyltransferase (COMT) inhibitors* (Comtan, Ongentys), *anticholinergics* (Cogentin, trihexyphenidyl), *amantadine*
- *Deep brain stimulation*
- *Focused ultrasound*—currently in clinical trials

*Side effects of medication—my experience*

- Extreme headaches
- Extreme fatigue
- Really bad nausea
- Constant constipation

- Dizziness
- Blood pressure problems
- Vision issues, dry eyes from not blinking as much
- Later on, the longer you are on medication and the more you take, additional issues arise

## Prevention

You can't prevent something when there is no known cause. I read somewhere that there is research currently being done for a possible vaccine that could prevent one from getting this dreadful disease. I honestly don't see how a vaccine will be of any use when there is no conclusive proof on how one gets the disease. Perhaps if you can conclusively prove that there is a genetic link and drill down, you might find a common chromosome or gene, then a vaccine can be created, targeting those who have it, based on genetics.

## Statistics (www.Parkinson.org)

- Nearly one million people in the US are living with Parkinson's disease (PD), which is more than the combined number of people diagnosed with multiple sclerosis, muscular dystrophy, and Lou Gehrig's disease (or amyotrophic lateral sclerosis). This is expected to rise to 1.2 million by 2030.
- Approximately 60,000 Americans are diagnosed with PD each year.
- More than ten million people worldwide are living with PD.

## Diagnosis

The standard diagnosis of Parkinson's disease right now is clinical, experts explain at

Johns Hopkins. That means there's no test, such as a blood test, that can give a conclusive result. Instead, certain physical symptoms need to be present to qualify a person's condition as Parkinson's disease. (www.hopkinsmedicine.org)

This is only a small list of the famous people who have or have died from Parkinson's. The list is long (www.Parkinson.org).

- Michael J. Fox
- Muhammad Ali
- George Bush
- Neil Diamond
- Ozzy Osbourne
- Pope John Paul II
- Janet Reno
- Linda Ronstadt
- Robin Williams (Lewy body)

# CHAPTER 2

—⚏—

# Child Abuse

*Definition of child abuse*

The Federal Child Abuse Prevention and Treatment Act (CAPTA) (42 U.S.C.A. § 5106g), as amended by the CAPTA Reauthorization Act of 2010, defines child abuse and neglect as, at minimum:

- Any recent act or failure to act on the part of a parent or caretaker, which results in death, serious physical or emotional harm, sexual abuse or exploitation; or
- An act or failure to act which presents an imminent risk of serious harm.
- This definition of child abuse and neglect refers specifically to parents and other caregivers. A "child" under this definition generally means a person who is younger than age 18 or who is not an emancipated minor.

While Federal legislation sets minimum standards for States that accept Federal funding, each State is responsible for defining child maltreatment in State law. Definitions of child abuse and neglect are typically located in two places within each State's statutory code:

- *Civil statutes* provide definitions of child maltreatment to guide individuals who are mandated to identify and report suspected child abuse and determine the grounds for intervention by State child protection agencies and civil courts.
- *Criminal statutes* define those forms of child maltreatment that can subject an offender to arrest and prosecution in criminal courts.

Many States recognize four major types of maltreatment in their definitions: neglect, physical abuse, sexual abuse, and emotional abuse or neglect. (www.childwelfare.gov)

## *What we know* (www.Focusonthefamily.com, www.MayoClinic.org)

"The truth is that most child abuse occurs inside the home of the victim."

"In many cases, child abuse is done by someone the child knows and trusts—often a parent or other relative."

"Many people are still reluctant to believe a child when they reveal abuse. One reason is that the behavior of some children who are abused, which is a trauma that affects them emotionally and physically, can give adults the impression that their word can't be trusted."

"Another reason can be when the person knows the parents or suspected abuser and finds it hard to believe the person is capable of such an act."

## Types of abuse (www.MayoClinic.org)

- *Physical abuse.* Physical child abuse occurs when a child is purposely physically injured or put at risk of harm by another person.
- *Sexual abuse.* Sexual child abuse is any sexual activity with a child, such as fondling, oral-genital contact, intercourse, exploitation, or exposure to child pornography.
- *Emotional abuse.* Emotional child abuse means injuring a child's self-esteem or emotional well-being. It includes verbal and emotional assault—such as continually belittling or berating a child—as well as isolating, ignoring, or rejecting a child.
- *Medical abuse.* Medical child abuse occurs when someone gives false information about an illness in a child that requires medical attention, putting the child at risk of injury and unnecessary medical care.

## Symptoms

A child who's being abused may feel guilty, ashamed, or confused. He or she may be afraid to tell anyone about the abuse, especially if the abuser is a parent, other relative or family friend. That's why it's vital to watch for red flags, such as:

- Withdrawal from friends or usual activities

- Changes in behavior—such as aggression, anger, hostility or hyperactivity—or changes in school performance
- Depression, anxiety or unusual fears, or a sudden loss of self-confidence
- An apparent lack of supervision
- Frequent absences from school
- Reluctance to leave school activities, as if he or she doesn't want to go home
- Attempts at running away
- Rebellious or defiant behavior
- Self-harm or attempts at suicide (www.MayoClinic.org)

## Complications of abuse

Some children overcome the physical and psychological effects of child abuse, particularly those with strong social support and resiliency skills who can adapt and cope with bad experiences. For many others, however, child abuse may result in physical, behavioral, emotional or mental health issues—even years later. Below are some examples.

- *Physical issues*
  - Premature death
  - Physical disabilities
  - Learning disabilities
  - Substance abuse
  - Health problems, such as heart disease, immune disorders, chronic lung disease and cancer

- *Behavioral issues*
  - Delinquent or violent behavior
  - Abuse of others
  - Withdrawal
  - Suicide attempts or self-injury
  - High-risk sexual behaviors or teen pregnancy
  - Problems in school or not finishing high school
  - Limited social and relationship skills
  - Problems with work or staying employed

- *Emotional issues*
  - Low self-esteem
  - Difficulty establishing or maintaining relationships
  - Challenges with intimacy and trust
  - An unhealthy view of parenthood
  - Inability to cope with stress and frustrations
  - An acceptance that violence is a normal part of relationships

- *Mental health disorders*
  - Eating disorders
  - Personality disorders
  - Behavior disorders
  - Depression
  - Anxiety disorders
  - Post-traumatic stress disorder (PTSD)
  - Sleep disturbances
  - Attachment disorders (www.MayoClinic.org)

# CHAPTER 3

—✺—

# Depression and Anxiety

*What is depression?*

Depression (major depressive disorder) is a common and serious medical illness that negatively affects how you feel, the way you think and how you act. Depression causes feelings of sadness and/or a loss of interest in activities you once enjoyed. It can lead to a variety of emotional and physical problems and can decrease your ability to function at work and at home.

Depression affects an estimated one in 15 adults (6.7%) in any given year. And one in six people (16.6%) will experience depression at some time in their life. Depression can occur at any time, but on average, first appears during the late teens to mid-20s. Women are more likely than men to experience depression. Some studies show that one-third of women will experience a major depressive episode in their lifetime. There is a high degree of heritability (approximately 40%) when first-degree relatives (parents/children/siblings) have depression. (www.psychiatry.org)

## What is anxiety?

*Anxiety* is an emotion characterized by feelings of tension, worried thoughts and physical changes like increased blood pressure. People with anxiety disorders usually have recurring intrusive thoughts or concerns. They may avoid certain situations out of worry. They may also have physical symptoms such as sweating, trembling, dizziness or a rapid heartbeat. (www.apa.org)

## Can someone have both depression and anxiety?

Depression and anxiety are different conditions, but they commonly occur together. Anxiety may occur as a symptom of clinical (major) depression. It's also common to have depression that's triggered by an anxiety disorder, such as generalized anxiety disorder, panic disorder or separation anxiety disorder. Many people have a diagnosis of both an anxiety disorder and clinical depression. (www.mayoclinic.org)

## Current treatments of depression and anxiety (www.psychiatry.org, www.webmd.com)

- Counseling—psychotherapy.
- Electroconvulsive therapy (ECT) is a medical treatment that has been most commonly reserved for patients with severe major depression, who have not responded to other treatments.
- Self-help by exercising, eating healthy, and getting regular sleep.
- Meditation.

- Most used medications are as follows:

  - Selective serotonin reuptake inhibitors (SSRIs), such as *citalopram (Celexa)*, *escitalopram oxalate (Lexapro)*, *fluoxetine (Prozac)*, *fluvoxamine (Luvox)*, *paroxetine HRI (Paxil)*, and *sertraline (Zoloft)*.
  - Selective serotonin and norepinephrine inhibitors (SNRIs), such as *desvenlafaxine (Khedezla)*, *desvenlafaxine succinate (Pristiq)*, *duloxetine (Cymbalta)*, *levomilnacipran (Fetzima)*, and *venlafaxine (Effexor)*.
  - *Vortioxetine (Trintellix* formerly *Brintellix)* and vilazodone *(Viibryd)* are newer medicines that both acts as SSRIs and also affect other serotonin receptors.
  - Tetracyclic *antidepressants* that are noradrenergic and specific serotonergic *antidepressants* (NaSSAs), such as *Remeron*.
  - Older *tricyclic antidepressants*, such as *Elavil*, *imipramine (Tofranil)*, *nortriptyline (Pamelor)*, and *Sinequan*.
  - Drugs with unique mechanisms such as *bupropion (Wellbutrin)*.
  - Monoamine oxidase inhibitors (MAOIs), such as *isocarboxazid (Marplan)*, *phenelzine (Nardil)*, *selegiline (EMSAM)*, and *tranylcypromine (Parnate)*.
  - N-methyl-D-aspartate (NMDA) Receptor Antagonist, such as *esketamine (Spravato)*
  - While not technically considered a medication by the FDA, *l-methylfolate (Deplin)* has proven successful in *treating depression*. It is categorized as a medical food or nutraceutical, requires a prescription and is the active form of a B-vitamin called folate. L-methylfolate helps regulate the neurotransmitters that control *moods*. (www.webmd.com)

# CHAPTER 4

## Childhood Bullying

As early as kindergarten, I can remember being picked on and bullied by my classmates. You see, I grew up in a small town called Paris, Missouri with a population of approximately 1,100. The town is very small, and everyone knows everybody. Paris reminds me of Walnut Grove in the *Little House on the Prairie* by Laura Ingalls. The shopkeeper, Mrs. Olsen, makes it her business to know what everyone in town was doing. Well, Paris has many Mrs. Olsens. There is nothing you can do without someone knowing it. Her daughter, Nelly, is the town bully and looks down her nose at everyone. She believes she is better than everyone else in the town. Well, like Mrs. Olsen and her spoiled snob of a daughter, Paris has many residents like the two of them. I don't mean any disrespect, and I am not claiming that everyone in my hometown was like them—I am just trying to draw a picture of the kind of place my hometown was when I lived there.

Living in a small town also had its advantages. One of the advantages is that the town will come together and help if a member of their community needs it. Kind of like when Charles Ingalls was injured in *Little House on the Prairie*—the community rallied around and helped him so that he would not lose his farm. My hometown would also do this for one of their own.

The problem, as I remember it, was that the parents of my classmates looked down on my family. You see, we didn't have much money and were considered lower class. Kids, unfortunately, will take cues from their parents. If the parents don't like the parents of a classmate, then the children won't associate with the children of those parents, which was pretty much my situation. I did have a few friends, but they were mostly people younger than me. It wasn't until my senior year that I was able to have a couple of friends that were my age and in my class.

Now that you have a general idea of my hometown and its residents, I will tell you how I was bullied. Back in kindergarten, this was when I really got an idea of how cruel other children can be. As a baby, my hair was blond. Well, by the time I got to kindergarten, my hair was turning red. As it was changing, it turned into a bright orange. Kids started calling me the class clown, Ronald McDonald. "You are so ugly, no one wants to be your friend."

One day at recess, I was hanging upside down on the monkey bars. I fell off and broke my arm; well, at least at that time, I thought I fell off. But the real reason I fell wasn't that I was clumsy and careless and fell off—it was because I was pushed, and it wasn't until my senior graduation that I found out who pushed me.

The bullying and name-calling continued and increased in intensity throughout my school years. Because once I hit puberty, I got really bad acne and I also had to wear glasses. Because we were poor, I had to wear glasses that were way big to fit my face. So now, I got called pumpkin head, pizza face, four-eyes, you name it—any horrible name they could call me, they did. I was always picked last during physical education or for any school activities.

In middle school, I believe it was seventh grade, I was walking home from school, and one of my male classmates named Jason came running after me with a few of his friends. He found much pleasure in calling me names and mocking me in front of his friends. Before it was all said and done, he shoved me to the ground as hard as he could. I was understandably upset. I went home all dirty like I had been in a fight. Well, I had to explain to my parents what had happened. My dad was so upset that he went to find the boy and, from my understanding, told him if he ever laid a hand on me again, he would have to deal with him. The boy never came near me again.

It was around this same time that I started dating a boy named Charles. Charles was a few years older than me and had his driver's license. Charles, as far as I knew, never knew of the abuse at home. I know that I never mentioned it. It was great having a boyfriend during this time in my life because, as long as Charles was at my house or I was with him somewhere, I didn't have to deal with my situation at home. I dated Charles until early in my sophomore year. We broke up before all hell broke loose at home. The timing of our breakup coincided with the timing of the Division of Family Services being called. This will be discussed further in the child abuse chapter.

Now, to graduation—the day I found out who pushed me off the monkey bars. Well, at graduation, we had to line up by last names in alphabetical order. Well, guess whom I got paired with? Chad, the kindergarten bully. As we were walking down the aisle to get to our seats, Chad, in a very hateful voice, told me what he had done that day in kindergarten. It was clear this wasn't an apology; he was making it clear that he still didn't like me. To this day, I have no idea what I have done to make him hate me so much as to cause me bodily harm. Also, as time passed, you would have thought his hate for me would have diminished some. Clearly not!

**Note to parents reading this**. Parents, teach your children to be nice to people that are different from them. Don't assume that they should know better. More and more, we are hearing on the news of school shootings. Kids nowadays are using violence to express their anger or frustrations that come from either being bullied in school or because they, like me, were also having issues at home. It is bad enough as a young person hitting puberty and all the emotions that come with that, to being bullied at school. Then they get home and have to deal with the abuse there. Even a strong person has their limits.

If you want the shootings to stop, then, as parents, you need to educate yourself and know the warning signs of a child in distress. Because ignoring the situation, thinking things will improve or go away in time, may come at a cost later.

## Childhood bullying statistics

Bullying statistics are alarming:

- 282,000 students are physically attacked in secondary schools each month
- 56% of students have personally witnessed some type of bullying at school
- 71% of students report incidents of bullying as a problem at their school
- Students in lower grades report being in twice as many fights as those in higher grades. However.
- There is a lower rate of serious violent crimes in the elementary level than in the middle or high schools
- 90% of 4th through 8th graders report being victims of bullying
- 30 percent of students are either bullies or victims of bullying (reported by ABC News)
- 1 in 7 Students in Grades K-12 is either a bully or a victim of bullying
- American schools harbor approx. 2.1 million bullies and 2.7 million of their victims. (Dan Olweus, National School Safety Center)
- 160,000 kids stay home from school every day due to fear of bullying (National Education Association & ABC News)
- 15% of all school absenteeism is directly related to fears of being bullied at school
- 1 of every 10 students who drops out of school does so because of repeated bullying (arkofhopeforchildren.org)


## Bullying and suicide

- Suicide is the third leading cause of death among young people—about 4,400 per year

- For every suicide among young people, there are at least 100 attempts—about 440,000!
- 14+% high school students have considered suicide, and almost 7% have attempted it
- Bully victims are 2–9 times more likely to consider suicide (Yale University study)
- At least half of suicides among young people are related to bullying (British study)
- 10–14-year-old girls may be at higher risk for suicide (arkofhopeforchildren.org)

# CHAPTER 5

# My Story
# Child Abuse, Physical

Now, we are getting to the part of the story that I have most dreaded writing. As much as I want to tell my story, a part of me is scared to tell my story. The fear of judgment, the embarrassment, and the telling of the story bring up many things I have long since kept buried. I also don't want to put a rift in the relationship that I am now trying to build with my parents.

If I am being honest, I am not 100 percent certain that I have remembered every incident that has happened to me. As a child, who is in pain, you try as hard as you can to block any memories of things that scare you or that bring up too much pain that your brain is unable to process. It is a protection mechanism because remembering everything is just too traumatic.

When did the abuse start? That is a good question. I know that I was really young.

When I was young and did something wrong, I just didn't get a spanking or a time-out, nor was I even sent to my room. Instead, I got a beating.

When I was perhaps four, maybe five, somehow, I found a book of matches. My younger self, not knowing any better, took the book of matches to our gravel driveway and was playing with them when my dad caught me. He yanked me up, brought me in, and beat me with his belt. You have to know that, when Dad beat me with his belt, it was never just with the leather portion of that belt; he had a huge metal belt buckle on it that he used. It was what always caused me the most pain.

Another one of the most memorable beatings I got—I don't remember what I did or exactly how old I was. I know I was a teenager. You know how this age group can be. At this stage, you get to the age where you think you are invincible and start challenging your parents. At least I did. I am fairly certain that I talked back to my father. Well, that was a mistake. This incident caused me one of the two beatings, the kind where I was fairly certain that he would have killed me had Mom not kept begging him to stop. My dad beat me so bad that day that I couldn't sleep on my back for several days.

I think you get the idea. I will mention this one last beating incident because it is important. I was in high school. This time, my father wasn't so careful. He was so angry at me that he punched me in the face several times. I wore glasses, so they got mashed into my face and went flying across the room. This time, there was no hiding the bruises, not even makeup was going to hide this beating. Both of my eyes were swollen shut. I had to miss school for a few days to let the swelling go down. When I went back to school, I remember my home economics teacher questioning me. Of course I was terrified and said nothing. My parents were called to school and questioned. As I mentioned previously, I had a boyfriend at this time, and we had recently broken up. My dad, when questioned, said my boyfriend and I got in a fight, and he did this to me. They didn't believe this, and the Department of Family Services was contacted.

I remember this like it was yesterday. My parents set us girls down at the kitchen table and explained that Family Services was coming to question us. We were told to say nothing or they would take us away and our father would go to jail. In fear of what would happen to us, we kept quiet.

By the way, this wasn't my dad's only incident, which made the excuse my parents said happened to me even less believable. One night, we went to the town fair with our father. Our mother wasn't there. I can't remember where she was. Our neighbor's daughter was at the fair alone. I remember my dad asking her if she needed a ride home. She took him up on his offer. After all, he was a neighbor and he had his kids with him—what could possibly happen, right?

Well, that was a mistake. Sometimes, the bad guy is a person you know. As soon as we got home, our father sent us girls directly to bed. I remember going to my room to get undressed and ready for bed. For some reason that I can't recall now, I left my room, and as I turned the corner, I saw my father completely naked, except for his underwear, and our neighbor dressed and completely horrified. At the sight of seeing me, she took the opportunity to escape and ran as fast as she could out of our house like the devil was chasing her.

The next morning, the police showed up. My father ended up going to court over the incident. I remember being told that I must say that I was in bed and didn't see anything. My father claimed that his brother, who lived with us a short time, was there that night and that he was with him the whole time. This was completely false. I assumed because I was a child, I was never interviewed or asked to testify. Our neighbor lost the case and moved away shortly after that.

# CHAPTER 6

## My Story
## Child Abuse, Sexual

Just when you think there couldn't possibly be more, well, there was. This was where everything went crazy for me. By the end of my story, I will have had a nervous breakdown, been handcuffed, and been taken to a mental hospital. Yes, you heard that right. I was sent to a mental hospital for evaluation.

This is the part of the story that I don't like to remember. The events leading up to me going to the mental hospital sent me into a very deep spiral—one that, to this day, I have not gotten over. I have much resentment and anger toward my family because of this single event. Forgiveness is the easy part; forgetting is a completely different story.

I really don't know how to write this portion of my story. Being abused by my father physically and being bullied by my classmates took a back seat to the sexual abuse. The very people you are supposed to count on in this cruel world and look up to are your parents and your relatives. But what does one do when the very people in this world that are supposed to protect you hurt you?

I am not certain at what age I was when I realized what my father did was wrong. Your dad touching you in intimate places is not exactly something you bring up when talking to the few friends you have. I think, deep in my gut, I always knew that this couldn't be right, and if it was right, why was it such a secret? I want to say this up front. My father never had sexual intercourse with us; we were not raped. What Dad did to us was fondle us in our private, most intimate areas. He also wanted us to see and touch him in his private, most intimate area. When my father did this, he was most often drunk. During most of my childhood, our father was a really bad alcoholic.

My father often took us to our local bar while he drank. Looking back now, I wonder why he took us, instead of leaving us at home. I mean, surely, leaving us home alone couldn't have looked anymore worse than taking us to the bar with him.

My father would get so drunk that there were many times when I remember him getting into fights and using foul language with other people in the bar. People in the bar offered to take us home when he was too drunk to drive, but he always refused. If they tried stopping him from leaving, a fight would happen. I remember one incident when he was so drunk that if I hadn't grabbed the wheel when I did, we would have hit several parked cars and would have driven off the road into a very deep ditch.

There were several incidents when, after we left the bar and got home, our father would expose himself and touch himself in front of us girls. If one of us girls didn't stay in the room while he did this, he would get really upset. You have to understand that we witnessed our father's anger in the bar, and we were too scared to say or do anything other than comply.

In my young and inexperienced mind, it never occurred to me that Dad was fondling my sisters in private like he was with me. Looking back, that was rather stupid of me because if he was exposing himself to all of us girls when we were together, why wouldn't he be doing something to them in private? The longer time elapsed with Dad never getting caught, the more confident he was getting. What I mean by that is that dad would often take us girls camping. While Mom was in the camper, Dad would be fondling my breasts right out in the open. I was too scared of him to yell or fight back, and when I did fight back in the past, a beating would happen. I often prayed that someone would come to our site and see him. It was always at night in the campground when he would do this, so unless you walked into our campsite, you wouldn't see anything. Mom never came out and caught him. Mom never was one for camping and would often stay in our air-conditioned camper and read and rarely came out.

By the time I began high school, I was really starting to realize that what Dad did wasn't normal. The last straw for me was, one day, I came home from doing something and I couldn't find my father or my sisters. I knew he was there because his truck was outside. My parents' bedroom was in our basement because they had remodeled it a couple of years before. I don't know why, but I was feeling really sick to my stomach, and my gut was warning me that something wasn't right.

I went downstairs to my parents' room to find it was locked from the inside. I really felt sick then because I just knew my sisters were in there, and I was right. Once they appeared out of the bedroom, I took them to another room, and I asked them if Dad did things to them in there, and they said yes. I made the decision to tell Mom right then and there. When my father did things to me in private, it was bad enough, but my fear for my sisters' well-being was my breaking point. I knew that I only had a few more years and I would be old enough to move out, and as long as I knew that my sisters were safe, then I would have just gone on with my life, not telling anyone. Since I had been the only one that my father abused physically, I thought I was the only one that he was fondling. That day changed everything.

My sisters and I told Mom that evening. My mom was in shock, as anyone would be. I thought Mom would have taken us away from that house that day because I didn't know what my father would do to us if he found out we told on him. Boy, was I shocked! Mom stayed. Life continued on for a little while at least.

You have to understand that our Mom was a victim as much as we were. My father was emotionally abusive to our mother as well as a drunk and a cheater. Some of my earliest memories were of my father calling Mom a worthless fat pig. "No one will want you. You need to stop eating before you get fatter than you already are." Then when she would stop eating, he would yell and scream at her for not eating. It was like he didn't want her fat but didn't want her skinny either. If she were skinny, she might leave him.

At first, I blamed my mom, just like you probably do right now. But you have to understand my mom had never been on her own and didn't even know how to pump her own gas. My grandfather owned a gas station and had always pumped the gas for her or my father did. I am not excusing her from her actions, but she isn't the only one who could have stepped in. My grandparents could have, other members of the family could have, but no one wanted to believe my father could do such a horrific thing.

Well, life went on. By this time, I was sixteen and could get a job. A job was a way to avoid my father. For some reason, our mother was never home. I continued cooking our meals, doing the laundry, cleaning the house, and doing homework before or after I got off to work. As long as I wasn't home, then nothing could happen, right? The guilt for leaving my sisters with him was horrible, but I knew if I was ever going to get out of this home, I needed to have a job and transportation. I decided to join the Navy once I graduated.

Shortly before the beating incident, noted in the "Physical Abuse" chapter, my long-term boyfriend, Charles, and I broke up. I am not sure if he ever knew that Dad blamed him for that beating incident. I doubt the police questioned him because no one believed my father's story anyway. We went on our separate ways, and I never told him about the abuse, physically or sexually. He liked my dad. Charles and my father often did things together, so I was never going to say anything. Not sure he would have believed me anyway.

By this time, I was really starting to exhibit signs listed in chapter 2. I was angry, bitter, rebellious, sleeping around—you name it. Pretty much everything but doing drugs. Of course it was this very kind of behavior that kept people from believing it happened once it came out.

Well, I guess you are wondering how I ended up with a nervous breakdown. I was seventeen and now dating a guy, Robbie, who lived in a small town about thirty minutes from my hometown. We got in a huge fight over the phone. I don't even remember what the fight was about. Something must have been in my voice that day because it is the only way I can explain how fast he made it to our house. I swear it seemed like only a few minutes and he was there. My father heard our fight, and he thought he would take advantage of the situation and use his method.

Something in me snapped. I grabbed the first thing I saw, which just happened to be a butter knife. I have no idea why I thought that it would protect me. At that moment, I just didn't care anymore. When Robbie came in, he saw me backed into a corner with the knife in my hand and my father walking toward me. I never saw Robbie that angry. He took my shocked father and threw him across the room. I panicked; I wasn't thinking clearly at that moment, so I ran. Where I was going by foot, I had no idea other than I had to get out of that house. By the time I came back out of the fog I was in, I realized that I couldn't go anywhere without my things.

When I got back to the house, Robbie was gone, and the police were there. I was handcuffed and taken to the nearest mental hospital for an evaluation. I was so confused—why was I being handcuffed and not my father? When I got to the mental facility, my parents were already there, telling the caseworker or psychologist about how I went crazy and tried killing my father. I tried explaining that this wasn't the case at all. Mom wasn't even there. Yes, I had a knife, a butter knife. The knife wasn't in my hand with the intent to kill anyone; it was there for protection to keep my father away from me. No one believed me, they just thought I was another troubled teen. While I was indeed troubled and needed help, I was the victim, not my father, as it was made to appear that day.

I panicked. I thought I was going to be locked up forever, so when no one was looking, I ran as fast as I could out of the hospital. I finally slowed down and had the sense to knock on someone's door to see if I could call my grandfather. He would believe me and protect me, right? How wrong I was. My grandfather showed up all right and took me back to the hospital. I was completely heartbroken. If even my grandfather didn't believe me, who would?

I was also upset and disappointed because by this time, I had plans to join the Navy. With me in the mental hospital, it would probably blow my one-and-only chance of getting out of this town and far away from my family.

The next morning, I was called to a conference room and seated around the table with what I could only assume were psychologists. I told them my story—all of it. I let it all out—the physical and sexual abuse. I told them about the neighbor girl, and I told them about Dad hitting on the few female friends I had at that time. I mean, why not? They wouldn't believe me anyway. None of my relatives did.

I couldn't have been more wrong. Later, as I was to find out, my sisters were brought in and questioned. They admitted everything. I often wonder if the friends I had at that time were questioned—after all, my father had made passes at them as well.

Suicide was something I had considered several times and attempted in my youth. One time, I actually took a whole bottle of pills. I never told anyone what I did. I don't know if anyone ever wondered where that bottle of pills went. The reason no one knew was that I couldn't keep down any of the pills I had taken. I think that this was God's work. It wasn't my time, so he was preventing this from happening. I will talk more about how God fits into my story in a later chapter.

## *Perpetrator statistics*

- About 90% of children who are victims of sexual abuse know their abuser.
- Only 10% of sexually abused children are abused by a stranger
- Approximately 30% of children who are sexually abused are abused by family members.
- The younger the victim, the more likely it is that the abuser is a family member. Of those molesting a child under six, 50% were family members.

- Family members also accounted for 23% of those abusing children ages 12 to 17.
- About 60% of children who are sexually abused are abused by people the family trusts.
- Homosexual individuals are no more likely to sexually abuse children than heterosexual individuals. (d2l.org)

## Long-term statistics of the sexually abused

- Adult women who were sexually abused as a child are more than twice as likely to suffer from depression as women who were not sexually abused.
- Adults with a history of child sexual abuse are more than twice as likely to report a suicide attempt.
- Females who are sexually abused are three times more likely to develop psychiatric disorders than females who are not sexually abused.
- Among male survivors, more than 70% seek psychological treatment for issues such as substance abuse, suicidal thoughts and attempted suicide.
- Women who were sexually abused as children were four times more likely than their non-abused peers to be diagnosed with an eating disorder.
- Middle-aged women who were sexually abused as children were twice as likely to be obese when compared with their non-abused peers. (d2l.org)

# CHAPTER 7

# *Family Life After It Became Public*

You would have thought now that everything was out, things would be better for my sisters and *me*. I guess, in many ways, yes, it was, as we wouldn't be abused anymore. I firmly believe that had we not come forward, our father would have eventually ended up raping one of my sisters. He most certainly wouldn't have quit drinking.

My sisters were taken in by our grandparents on my mother's side. I went into foster care. This is why I now currently suffer from abandonment issues. Thanks to kids making fun of me in school my whole life, I had very little self-confidence. I didn't believe I was lovable or even likable. When no one in my family stepped in to be my guardian, I was devastated. The family wanted my sisters but not me.

My mom stuck by my father, just as her own father said she should. He was old-fashioned and believed you should stay married for better or worse. Eventually, my mother got custody of my sisters. My grandparents had both gotten cancer and later passed away—first, my grandmother, then a few years later, my grandfather. Our mother used a majority of the money she inherited to keep my father out of prison. Our house went up for auction. Mom's money was gone, and my father ended up leaving our mother for my now-stepmom.

Our father had numerous affairs and had gotten one of the women pregnant. This is when my brother comes into the picture. In one of the earlier chapters, I mentioned my father yanking the phone out of the wall. This was the night, I believe, Mom found out about the affair and about my brother. This was when Mom left. She left without us. She later told us she couldn't afford to take us. Living in a small town of 1,100 people, there just weren't any jobs.

I know many of you will be saying that she could have found a way and that she should have never left her children with the man she knew had abused them—it is easy to judge, but none of us can know what we will do until put into that situation. Also, as I mentioned before, my mother was also a victim, and my father's emotional abuse at that time was bad. He made her believe that she couldn't make it without him, much less take care of us girls.

I mentioned earlier that I ended up in foster care. My boyfriend, Robbie, came to my rescue again. Both he and his mom offered to take me in. They also helped me become emancipated so that I could be free of the foster system. I owe my life to this family. They took me in when none of my relatives did, they made me feel welcome, and they never spoke of why I was there. Even when my boyfriend Robbie and I couldn't make the relationship work, they never disrespected me. Robbie and I remained friends until his death.

If I ever won the lottery, I would love to set up a foundation in his name. I am not sure if Robbie ever told his wife and children what he and his mom did for me when I was seventeen. If not, if they read this, I want them to know that her husband and their father was a hero to me, and I will never forget Robbie and his mother's kindness to me when everyone else turned their backs.

After Robbie and I broke up, I struggled financially. It is hard living on your own, especially at seventeen. I had a year before the Navy would be able to swear me in. So during this time, I couch-surfed at my friends' houses. I slept in my vehicle. One of my uncles finally said I could stay with him for a while. He didn't know how to deal with me. I was fifty shades of fu—— up by this time. I was hurt, couldn't trust anyone, and rebellious as hell. When I overstayed my welcome there, I went to live with another uncle. This situation as well didn't work out. He had children, and my rebellious nature wasn't setting a very good example to them.

It was now 1989. I was eighteen. I was to be sworn into the Navy on July 11 (if I remember correctly). Before I enlisted, I met my soon-to-be husband on June 3, a little more than a month before I was to go to boot camp. As planned, I was sworn in, and off to Orlando, Florida, boot camp I went. My boyfriend and I kept in touch through letters. My stint in the Navy didn't last long. I had health issues and mental health issues at this time. I was to be medically discharged but opted to get out under a general discharge. They couldn't tell me how long the medical discharge would take, and I felt that I was needed at home. During this time, my father's trial was beginning. I wanted to be there in case my sisters needed me, and I had also hoped that I would be called upon to give my testimony.

By the time I got back though, it was too late. The trial had ended with my father pleading guilty to two charges of sodomy to minors, and he had to register as a sex offender for the rest of his life. Because of him pleading guilty and because he had some people speak up on his behalf, he was released for a time he already spent while waiting for trial. He was also required to get counseling.

# CHAPTER 8

## Life After Father's Conviction

This part of my story is where I hope that I don't skip around much. I am going to start this portion of my story sometime after our father's conviction, as mentioned in the previous chapter. I feel that revisiting the past helps you better understand me and my current situation and state of mind.

It was 1994. Both my middle sister and I had become pregnant. She had a son, and I had a daughter two months and two weeks after she delivered. After I gave birth to our daughter, I had frequent nightmares. I feared that what happened to me would happen to our daughter. I was terrified to leave her anywhere there would be a man in the house. I was also terrified of leaving her with my husband's family. I was so terrified when I left her with my husband's family that I just couldn't enjoy myself when I went out. As time passed, I found it easier and easier to let my husband go out while I stayed at home. My husband's family didn't give me any reason to think they couldn't be trusted; it was just my fear talking. I knew that my brain wouldn't be able to cope should something happen to her. I wasn't even supposed to have children, so my daughter was my miracle child. I swore to protect her, even if it meant losing my own life.

My middle sister, on the other hand, constantly left her boy, and later her two boys, with our father. I never understood how she could do that. By that time, we had already found out that our father had also abused our uncle. So our father didn't have a gender preference. My middle sister and I often fought about this. My middle sister often had to support her children alone because her ex couldn't be counted on to help support their children. He would go buy a gun or a bow and arrow before making sure that his children had everything they needed.

My middle sister often counted on our father to help support her children. She needed him financially, and because of this, she expected our father to be present at all of the holiday gatherings. Nearly every year, a fight would ensue between us. I didn't want him there, and she did. She often used bullying manipulative tactics to get her way. She would often use the threat—if he isn't invited then I wasn't invited, or if I had the gathering and he wasn't welcome, then her family wouldn't come. I often caved, which I now know was a mistake on my part. By me always caving, I was never able to heal or deal with the trauma.

Fast-forward to 2020. My middle sister bought a house with her long-term boyfriend, now husband. On a trip to St. Louis, my middle sister confided that she had started having nightmares. I believe that all of the trauma she experienced she had blocked out because it was the only way her brain could handle being around our father. Remember I mentioned she needed him financially? I don't find it surprising or a coincidence that her nightmares began right after she and her husband moved in together. She no longer needed our father's support. It was at this point that she started avoiding our father.

Several years prior to her moving in with her now-husband, our mother went to live with her. They both needed help financially. Mom was on disability by then and eventually on SSI. Because our mom never made much money, her monthly SSI checks aren't much, and it doesn't leave her much to live on. So financially, for the two of them, it made sense to move in and share expenses.

When my middle sister moved in with her husband, according to our mom, she still continued to pay some of the household expenses. Recently, this year 2022, Mom contracted COVID-19 and was hospitalized, and because of her already declining health, she had to go into skilled nursing for a while. Once again, my middle sister and I were back fighting with each other. My middle sister and I couldn't agree on Mom's care or with the financial aspects of Mom's current situation. My sister told me that I was an ungrateful daughter, and that I didn't love our mom if I couldn't financially help. I felt that my middle sister was placing my value on the family for financial need rather than love. My middle sister was telling anyone that would listen that I was an ungrateful daughter because I wouldn't financially help Mom. This told me exactly where I stood with her and Mom.

I had my own health to consider, and my middle sister's threats and her methods of manipulation by making me look like an ungrateful daughter wasn't going to work. I had to consider my own health and expenses. I didn't know how much longer I would be able to work, and I was not wealthy. I had $86,000 in student loans, I had to meet a $3,500 medical deductible each year, and I just had to borrow $8,000 to get my teeth fixed. It was not that I didn't want to help—I financially couldn't. When you have a chronic disease like mine, every year for the last seven years, I had to pay my high deductible and maximum out of my pocket. This didn't include the money I spent each year at the dentist or eye doctor. I just couldn't seem to catch a break.

Dawn has had enough. It is time to take care of Dawn. It is time to stop worrying about what other people think of me. Plus, I learned a long time ago not to count on anyone but myself. It is time. I take back control of my life. Those that want to be in my life will, and those that don't won't. I just have to trust that, this time, I won't be alone. Yes, the circle might be small and might get smaller as I progress, but I survived before without family support, and I will do so again. Nobody deserves to be made to feel bad for taking care of themselves first. Anybody who places a value on you based on how much financial support you give them doesn't value you as a person—they only value what you can give them. They don't deserve you anyway.

# CHAPTER 9

# Facebook

You are perhaps wondering how in the world Facebook can break up a family. You see, my father decided to join Facebook during the pandemic in 2021, not sure why, in his seventies, he wanted to. Perhaps because of boredom, or maybe so that he can have a way to keep in touch with his brother in Texas. Perhaps, too, because he is a registered sex offender and was concerned that he wouldn't be able to have an account, so he waited. Well, for any reason, his actions on Facebook opened up a lot of old wounds that had been left buried for years.

My father, being in his seventies now was not very knowledgeable about Facebook back then. But the more he was on it, the more he learned. Over the course of months, he started to learn how to share things with his Facebook friends. One day, he decided to share a post. This post basically said that sex offenders need to be locked up and never let out.

My sisters and I were speechless. I mean, after all, he is a registered sex offender himself. Because of his advanced age, him finding *God*, and because he had stopped drinking years before, we let this slide. We were not happy, but we wanted to keep the peace. Our father had found *God* and even believed he was his prophet, so we couldn't wrap our minds around the idea that he would lie to people on Facebook or anywhere. After all, how can you have an honest relationship with God and say you are his prophet if he was not honest with what he did to his children?

Fast-forward to July 4, 2021—this would have been my wedding anniversary. The man I met before I went into the Navy, I ended up marrying back in 1997. As my disease started progressing, the more depressed I became. I was having frequent nightmares of everyone leaving me when my health got bad. So I started pushing people away. I ended up asking for a divorce. I didn't really want a divorce—my husband and I had been together since June 3, 1989. I just wanted my husband to fight for our marriage, prove that he could handle my illness, tell me he loved me, and spend more time with me instead of with his friends every weekend. I was really scared, and I needed him now more than ever.

My husband and I, after the divorce, decided to stay together and try to work on things. I was deeply depressed between my disease and my family life, past and present. I felt like I lost everything. My marriage, my home that my husband received in the divorce, my health, and, to top it off, my father's disacknowledgment of what he did just kept getting under my skin and was causing me to have more and more nightmares. My health was deteriorating, and I was starting to feel that no one loved me, just like I felt no one loved me or was there for me in my childhood. I just couldn't shake this feeling of abandonment, even though I was the one pushing people away. I think, in my mind, that if I pushed everyone away, then no one would leave me—I left them.

I was so depressed. I was contemplating suicide. After all, if I killed myself, I wouldn't have to worry about who would stand by me through this progressive disease and leave me all alone or dump me in a nursing home. I just felt completely alone and unloved. My posts on Facebook were negative and were signaling that something was really wrong with me, and my father took notice. My youngest sister and I had already talked, and I told her that the loss of my marriage brought back old wounds of abandonment and that I feared that I would be going through this disease alone—like I went through our childhood alone—when my health continues to get worse.

My father contacted my sister by text, asking what was wrong with me. She told him that I was struggling with what he did to us girls all those years ago and the abandonment I felt from the family. She also told him that he owed me an apology. He told her that he didn't know what she was talking about, that he never did anything to us girls, and he wished we could just forget the past and move on. Well, that didn't go over well with her. She later showed my middle sister, Mom, and me his text. This was when we girls decided to cut ties with our father. As of the date of this book, I haven't seen my father since before my incident on July 4, 2021.

When my little sister showed me our father's text, I lost it. I had enough of pretending all was well in our family. I finally realized that our father was living his life as if nothing happened. Perhaps more jail time would have been needed for him to contemplate what he did and what his actions would cost us in the future.

All of us girls, as an adult, were struggling with the ramifications of his behavior when we were children. We were having nightmares. For years, I was living with the belief that our father was a changed man. He quit drinking and found God, as I mentioned in the previous chapter. As far as I knew, he had never touched another child, and in my head, I believed that he was drunk all of those times the incidents happened. If he would have been sober, none of those things would have happened.

One day, as usual, something kept nagging at me. Remember in my story what made us girls come clean all those years ago? It was the day our father had locked my sisters in his bedroom. I had this thought—*if our father was drunk, how could that bedroom door get locked? No way would my sisters lock themselves in that room.* It was this thought that made me finally realize he couldn't have been drunk during these incidents, and he, as a protection mechanism, was possibly blocking things out. But how many drunks do you know that would have the mindset to lock the door with their children in the room unless they intended to do something wrong? He must have known what he was doing was wrong, or he wouldn't have locked that door. So this meant my earlier belief that he was drunk no longer held true for me.

I lost it since our father wouldn't come clean and apologize and acknowledge to his wife and son what he did to us. Clearly, his talks with Jesus were lies. You can't repent your sins to Jesus when you can't and won't acknowledge and admit to the wrongs you have done.

This time, my eyes were finally opened. Our father was using Jesus as a coping mechanism because he feared he will go to hell when he dies. I had been living a lie all these years. I let my relationship with our father continue under the belief that he was sorry.

Because I had continued a relationship with my father, it led many people in our hometown, including members of our family, to believe that what Dad did never happened, that we girls were liars. I mean, why would people believe anything that happened, right? If something did happen, why would Dawn and the girls still have a relationship with him? I even moved in with him when I was homeless for a while. I had nowhere else to go, and he made sure not to be there when I was there. My current boyfriend, whom I ended up marrying, spent a lot of time with me there as well just to be sure.

I finally decided enough was enough. If I was ever going to heal, I had to come out publicly and acknowledge what he did to me and my sisters. I never got my day in court as my sisters had. I needed to tell my story, and I had to make sure that my father knew that enough was enough, that his past was about to catch up with him.

I went public on Facebook. I wanted to make it clear to him, our family, and my friends from my hometown on Facebook that I didn't lie all those years ago. He could make people doubt what happened when I was a child, especially when the oldest (me) had behavioral issues. Well, the same couldn't be said now that I was a fifty-year-old adult. That got him and others to take notice. My father, stepmom, and brother unfriended and blocked me. I expected that. While this didn't change all the emotional issues I was dealing with, coming clean and finally acknowledging what happened took a weight off my chest that I had been carrying for years. By not acknowledging publicly what had happened and by not having my day in court, I was making my father the victim and us girls liars. He wasn't the victim. He never was—us girls were.

It was disappointing that my brother blocked me, or maybe, he just didn't get on Facebook anymore. I didn't know. I did know that his mom and my father blocked me. What I would like my brother to understand is that by the time our father came into his life, my father wasn't the same man my sisters and I knew and grew up with. Would he think differently if our father had not changed and done something to his children?

I finally realized that I was not my parents. We each chose our own paths. We can't blame *God* or others. We can ride the merry-go-round forever or get off. I am choosing to get off.

Andrea Day's song "Rise Up" couldn't have said it any better.

> You're broken down and tired, of living life on the merry-go-round, and you can't find the fighter, but I see it in you, so we gonna walk it out Move mountains. We gonna walk it out, and move mountains, and I'll rise up. I'll rise like the day; I'll rise up, I'll rise unafraid, I'll rise up and I'll do it a thousand times again.

I just needed to put one foot in front of the other. I needed to take one day at a time. I am strong. I am a fighter. I made it this far. I can keep going.

# CHAPTER 10

## How Does God Fit into My Story

You might be wondering how God fits into my story.

1. God and my father
2. My faith

God plays an important part in my story. As I mentioned in my introduction, I stated that I have forgiven my father a long time ago. Yes, this is true. I have forgiven my father. At the time I am writing this, we are currently not speaking, but it isn't because I haven't forgiven him.

Let me explain. Just because you forgive someone doesn't mean that you forget what they did, nor does it mean that you should keep them in your life. If your relationship is toxic or causing you unnecessary stress, you have to separate yourself from the situation. The relationship between my father and my middle sister causes my blood pressure to rise and causes me too much stress for this reason alone. I had to separate myself from them.

For years, I kept the relationship with my family members due to obligation and because I felt that it made me a bad person if I didn't. In time, I have come to a realization that if I don't separate myself from those who cause stress in my life, then my health condition will rapidly progress faster than if I was to be in a much calmer stressless environment. This doesn't mean that I don't care or that I wish any harm to come to those I have removed from my life.

Now to God and my father—sometime after my father's conviction, he stopped drinking, smoking, and found peace with God. I am not sure if the conviction made him change or if it was something else entirely—it could be that he was getting older and he felt that if he didn't find God before he passed then he would end up in hell. It doesn't really matter what the reason was.

Because he found God, he became the man that we girls wish we had growing up. Our brother was lucky he got to know only the good side of our father. My sisters and I, as adults, got to see what our father would have been like if circumstances had been different.

Our father now believes he is one of Jesus's prophets. He believes that Jesus visits him regularly. Is he crazy, or might this be true? Well, I can't prove this one way or another. Who am I to say, and if this belief makes him feel better and keeps him on the straight and narrow path, then I say good for him because the alternative would have been worse.

My only real issue with his belief is that he lectures people constantly about repenting. While I am no saint and I have made my share of mistakes, the last thing I needed was a lecture from someone who has caused me and continued to cause me emotional stress. Also, as I mentioned earlier in my story, by not acknowledging what he did to us girls, he was not only lying to us and others, but this meant that he was lying to *God*. I know now he wasn't drunk; a drunk person would not have had the mental capacity, at that time, to lock that door, especially since that was not a habit that he had. Since he wasn't being truthful, he was committing a sin. I believe that *God* would want our father to be honest, not just to himself but to everyone. The *God* I believe in wouldn't promote a lie to him or to anyone. But this is between my father and God. Our father's admission of the truth is not going to undo the damage he caused to me or my sisters or to the neighbor girl—it would just give us the validation that we were and are being truthful about what happened.

To my readers who do not believe in *God*—I am not going to try to sway you, one way or the other. Each of us has our own beliefs, and I myself have wavered over the years. I mean, after all, why would *God* our Father, if he exists, allow bad things to happen to his children?

I do have an answer for this. He allows this because we were sent here to learn and to grow spiritually. Why would we leave the kingdom in heaven if our life in our physical body was supposed to be perfect? It would be like getting a master's degree without taking any courses. Also, *God* doesn't see death as a punishment, nor does he let things happen. We, as humans, make things happen. Just as guns don't kill people, people kill people. We need to stop blaming *God* for not stopping these horrible acts and put the blame where it belongs. Our time here is our classroom. We were sent here to learn then to return home. Death, or how you leave this place, is not a bad thing to *God*—it is a celebration of your return to him. Death only hurts us here because we let doubts set in and we scare ourselves into believing there is not a kingdom of heaven and we won't see our loved ones, who have passed on, ever again.

Let's face it—if *God* sent us here with our memories of heaven and what we would have to do to people to complete our mission, would you want to come here? If you knew all of the bad things that were going to happen to you in advance and the amount of pain you would experience or cause someone else, would you want to or be able to fulfill your mission?

I know what you are thinking. Here is another religious fanatic trying to push *God* onto them. First off, I do not regularly go to church, nor do I read my Bible religiously. I couldn't even quote a verse out of the Bible. My belief stems from what happened to me over twenty years ago. I even debated whether to mention this at all. I know people will think I am crazy and say it happened because of this or that. Could I have had Parkinson's back then? I can tell you that I *did not* have any symptoms of the disease at that time. The symptoms didn't appear until at max two years before diagnosis, which puts me at having the disease thirteen years ago at max. I will let you decide if what happened to me was real or a figment of my imagination.

Twenty years ago, I had a partial hysterectomy. Everything but one ovary was removed. Our daughter, at that time, was seven. Several days after the surgery, I fell asleep in our living room chair. I was waiting for our daughter to get off the school bus. You must know that I had not been taking any pain medication and the doctor had gotten on to me for not taking any. I don't handle pain medication well. I can't take codeine at all. I have had several surgeries in the past, and I fill the prescription, just in case, but I rarely take it. If I do, I have to be in extreme pain because my stomach just can't tolerate it. I get really sick. Since it had been several days after surgery, I can't even explain that what happened to me was because of the medication they used to put me under.

I fell asleep, as I said. The next thing I remember was a really bright white light. It was blinding. I couldn't see anything at all. I don't remember ever seeing anything but this bright white light, but I remember the voice and our conversation. I was talking to *God*. The voice didn't have to tell me this because I just knew. I wasn't scared. It was like I was used to having a conversation with him, even though I don't ever recall having one before.

During this conversation, I knew that I had left my body, just like I knew I was speaking to *God*. *God* asked me if I wanted to stay or return to my body. I told him that I wanted to come back and be there to raise our daughter. He told me that if I returned, my life would be difficult, even more so than before. He wouldn't tell me what in my life would be difficult, just that it wasn't going to be easy for me. He again asked me if I wanted to return, and I had to decide quickly because time was running out. What he meant by this was that we can only be gone from our physical bodies for a certain amount of time. If that window of time passed, it would be too late.

I told him yes—that no matter what, I wanted to return. He said *okay* but to remember it was my choice and always has been. The next thing I remember was that I was going really fast, and I kept repeating over and over to myself that I had to hurry. As I came to my physical body, I was struggling to get back in. I was starting to panic, thinking it had been too late. I could hear the TV in the background, but I couldn't see anything. I just kept trying. Then all of a sudden, I felt myself reenter my body. My panic subsided.

I never told anybody this story until a few years ago. I just knew people would think I was crazy. Shoot, I even thought I was crazy. Time went on, and I didn't give it another thought, not until I was diagnosed with Parkinson's anyway. Then my mind went back to that day twenty years ago and the conversation I had with *God*. It was then that I realized that perhaps I did talk to *God*. When *God* said my life wasn't going to be easy, was he talking about Parkinson's? After all, my life, up to this point, hadn't been easy, so what could possibly be worse? I think I had my answer.

*God* was trying to prepare me for what was to come. I got angry with him. I had a few choice words with him. I screamed at him. I said, "Why didn't you tell me it was going to be Parkinson's?"

I never got a response. I was very upset with *God*, and it took a few years before I would find *God* again.

I had to focus on my health. I went through a series of emotions—disbelief, anger, acceptance, disbelief again, then finally, my health was just too bad to ignore, so I had to fully accept what I had.

To date, I have not had another incident with *God* like the one I spoke of earlier. I have had several surgeries since and never had another instance like twenty years ago. I can tell you that each time I found myself in a deep cavern of depression, I felt that he was there. One time, I didn't think he was. It was after I finally had to accept what I had that I spiraled into a deep depression. All I could think of was what kind of financial situation I was going to be putting on my husband and daughter by having this disease. We were not rich, and we needed my income. Any SSI Disability I will get will go toward medical expenses, and eventually, I will qualify for Medicare, but how does one support themselves while waiting on SSI Disability and Medicare approval? I heard it can take years. Even after Disability acceptance, you don't qualify for Medicare until two years after you are deemed disabled by the Social Security Administration.

Until that happens, I still have to have insurance and be able to pay COBRA insurance, not counting the $3,500 maximum out-of-pocket deductible I have to meet. I also still have a vehicle payment and a student loan payment. I needed to have a vehicle to be able to get to appointments, or my husband or daughter will have to take off and risk their own jobs.

Anyway, this was all I could think about, worry about. I went to the park so I could have a private conversation with *God*—well, me more or less screaming at him. I was blaming him for my circumstances and my fear. I told him that I couldn't put this burden on my family, and unless he stepped up and prove to me that he was listening, then I would hopefully be joining him shortly.

I waited around for a while, waiting for a sign. Nothing! So I got up and left. I had already decided how I was going to do it. I got in my SUV, and when I turned the vehicle on, this song was playing: it was "Overcomer" by Mandisa. The very first words I heard come out of the radio were as follows:

> *God's* still there, even if you don't see him.
> Hold on a little while longer. Try to do the
> best you can. He knows it hurts. He will help you
> get through this, so hang on a little while longer.
> Stay in it until the final round.

If this wasn't a sign, then I don't know what is. I left the parking lot, bawling my eyes out.

I know what you are thinking, *why didn't* GOD *send a message to other people who committed suicide to prevent it from happening?* There could be two possible answers to this question. (1) He might have, but they might have thought they were hearing things or were too far gone to care. (2) I believe that we all have chosen how we will die before we come here, perhaps suicide was their predetermined path.

What I do know is that I tried committing suicide twice by swallowing a large number of pills when I was younger. Both times that I tried, I couldn't keep them down. I should have died, especially since I didn't tell anyone or ever go to the hospital to get my stomach pumped. Suicide must not have been my predetermined path, or I would have died.

Again, this story is about my experience, and it isn't being used as a tool to convince you that there is a *God*. Every person has to make that determination on their own. Just maybe, I imagined what happened to me, but if I did, it sure seemed real, and just as predicted, my life with Parkinson's has been anything but easy.

Even with my belief, when life gets tough, I often wonder if there was a *God*. I am sure a majority of people go back and forth when times get tough. There are many, like my father, who hide behind *God* to try to atone for their actions in their life. My father judges others, just as I mentioned earlier, when he posted on Facebook that sex offenders need to be locked up.

If he got better and found *God* and expects forgiveness, then he, too, must not judge and pray that the other people who have committed horrible acts also find *God* and are also forgiven. No matter how someone behaves, past or present, who am I to judge anyway? This book is not intended to judge anyone. I am simply telling my story to help me deal with my past. I also hope that my book is a comfort to others and that they know that they are not alone, that they don't have to hide anymore. Not talking about a tragedy in your life doesn't make it go away—believe me, I have tried. Your anger and resentment just fester and grow. I have had some really bad things happen to me, and it is only bound to get worse as the disease progresses.

I have a tattoo on my arm that says, "You got this. Stay strong." It is in the shape of a heart with a cross and an anchor. The cross symbolizes my faith, and the anchor is one of the first Christian symbols, and it symbolizes the hope of my salvation through Christ.

# CHAPTER 11

## *Diagnosis*

Before I describe what life is like with Parkinson's, let me discuss how I found out that I had this disease. My very first symptoms were not noticed by me. My best friend, Ann, noticed them. She said, "Dawn, I am concerned. Your pinky finger on your left hand is twitching, and I have noticed that you are slurring your speech and you are having balance issues."

I had fallen recently, so I thought that, maybe, I had some kind of nerve damage from the fall. I scheduled a visit with my general doctor as soon as I could. He did his evaluation and said, "Dawn, I am afraid that you don't have nerve damage. You have Parkinson's."

I was like "What?" I don't know what Parkinson's is other than Michael J. Fox has it. He gave a brief explanation and sent me on my way.

To say I was shocked was an understatement. My mind just couldn't process what I had just found out. I was thinking that he must be wrong I was too young for this disease. It must be something else. I decided to get a second opinion, so an appointment with a neurologist was scheduled. I went to this appointment, and he also confirmed the diagnosis. He said, "Dawn, there is no test you can take to prove with 100 percent accuracy that you have Parkinson's, but you exhibit many symptoms of the disease [tremors, small handwriting, balance issues, etc.]. I recommend you try some Parkinson's medication to see if it helps."

Well, I left the office still not convinced that I had it. I decided to forego medication at this point. After all, my symptoms were not that bad. I had researched Parkinson's and medication before I made my appointment. I knew how bad the side effects would be if you went on medication and that, the longer you were on it, the more you would need it until you get to the point where, along with the nasty side effects, long-term use will bring forth additional symptoms.

Over the course of years, I battled with disbelief, acceptance, and anger—emotions that one goes through when diagnosed with a chronic disease. I got to the point, almost five years ago, that I couldn't manage the symptoms anymore. I just couldn't deal with it anymore. Instead of just my pinking finger shaking, now my whole left side was on full vibration mode. I was having anxiety attacks. I had fallen again and could barely walk. So I scheduled another appointment with my neurologist and began medication treatment.

Oh my, those first three months on Sinemet were horrible. I had migraines. The nausea was so bad, and it was constant day in and day out. I thought that suffering from the side effects of the disease might be better than taking this medication. It was my uncle with Parkinson's who told me to stick it out, that the side effects would become more manageable with time. He was right. The side effects became manageable as time passed. The medication did help. If people look at me, I appear normal. The tremors, as long as I take the medication every three hours, are not noticeable unless you look for them.

My uncle with Parkinson's passed away in 2021. It was a sad and scary time for me. His death made me think of my own death. Death doesn't scare me now that I know and believe there is a *God*, but how you die and how long you suffer before it happens—those scare me.

# CHAPTER 12

## Living with the Disease

My life with Parkinson's. How do I even describe what living with this disease is like? Just imagine having constant draining fatigue and constantly having at least one or more symptoms of the disease that the medication doesn't help with.

If you were sick every day for weeks, not knowing when or if you would ever get over this sickness, by day two or three, you get grouchy right? This is what Parkinson's is like. Every day, it is something. Some days, you take your medication religiously at the same time, and sometimes, it works, and sometimes, it doesn't. You just never know what the new day will bring.

What I can constantly count on is fatigue, depression, vision issues due to dry eyes, and oh, boy, the pain. These four things never go away. The daily constant pain is the worst. My pain management specialist has tried to control it with pain medication and muscle relaxers, and I have gotten several steroid injections. The medication and shots managed the pain to a degree so that I can function and work, but it is never fully gone. Exercise is supposed to help slow progression, but every time I try to do more than walking, my body hurts so bad for two weeks after to the point that I can't sleep. So against the doctor's orders, I don't exercise—at least not much or enough.

I am not lazy. Before my pain progressed to the point where it is now, I was at a good weight for my build, and I loved to jog. I would jog three miles a day. I felt great. That was nearly seven years ago. Now, even just cleaning my house has become a chore. It hurts so bad when I try to clean our two bathrooms that I can barely stand when I am done. I would love to have someone come to clean my house, but unfortunately, with my current financial situation, I can't afford this on a regular basis.

## My symptoms and how it affects my daily life

- *Pain*—I talked about that above. Like I said earlier, the pain is never-ending and is all consuming. I am functional at best. I miss the gym and my daily three-mile jogs. I am now overweight due to no exercise and poor eating habits.
- *Sleeping*—it is something I now dread. I can only sleep upright because the pain is too severe if I push myself up when I need to use the restroom or to turnover. I had to buy an adjustable bed. Even with the adjustable bed, it hurts like hell by the time morning rolls around. Arthritis has set in on both my hips and in the middle of my back.
- *Vision*—it is a constant problem at work because with Parkinson's comes dry eyes. The dry eyes come from our inability to blink as often as we used to. Blinking keeps your eyes moist, and if your eyes become too dry, they burn like hell. I have issues seeing the rows in spreadsheets or using the computer for anything. I was prescribed medication to help with this, but the cost was too high, so I couldn't continue taking it.
- *Depression and anxiety*—this one is a major problem. Not everyone with Parkinson's has issues with this. I think mine is not just due to Parkinson's but due to childhood trauma as well. This has one has cost me my marriage, as well as issues when dealing with friends, family, and strangers.

I get so tired of people telling me to be positive. "You can be happy if you choose to be happy." They say happiness is a choice. While being happy is easy for some people, it isn't as easy for those of us with chronic health conditions or with brain conditions. There isn't an on or off switch, nor do I believe that people like me don't want to be happy. Depression and anxiety aren't something a person chooses. We just don't wake up one day and say, "I choose to be negative and unhappy, and I get some much enjoyment in being miserable." No!

There are many articles and studies done that state people with Parkinson's have very low levels of dopamine.

> Dopamine deficiency can cause a person to have feelings of apathy and fatigue and to suffer from mood swings and chronic boredom. However, dopamine deficiency can also cause major health problems like depression, various addictions, Attention Deficit Hyperactivity Disorder (ADHD) and Parkinson's disease. (healthyandnaturalworld.com)

I hate being depressed; it takes up a lot of my precious quality time. My brain just won't stop working, and it is constantly feeding me negative thoughts. For example, I sit and worry constantly about when I won't be able to walk anymore, work anymore, how I am going to pay my financial obligations when this happens. When I get a grandchild, will they be scared of me? Will I be able to hold him or her? I just can't shut it off, and when it gets bad, the anxiety kicks in. Once the anxiety kicks in, my tremors show themselves, and my body is like a large motor that is making the vehicle (my body) vibrate, which doesn't stop unless given medication or until you remove what caused the stress in the first place.

A couple of weeks ago, I went on Prozac for depression. I realized I couldn't handle this without some prescribed help. I hate admitting this because it makes me feel weak. I was miserable, and I just needed to swallow my pride and realize that I can take medication and still be strong. The medication doesn't define you; continuing to fight does.

If, like me, you are struggling in coping day to day, here are some songs that helped pull me from the brink of death. I hope that they help you as well. You are not alone.

My favorite songs are as follows:

- "Overcomer" by Mandisa
- "You're Gonna Be Okay" by Jenn Johnson
- "Fear Is a Liar" by Zach Williams
- "Survivor" by Zach Williams
- "Rise Up" Andra Day
- "Just Be Held" by Casting Crowns
- "Lies" by Lee Brice
- "In Jesus' Name" by Katy Nichole

- *Fatigue*—oh, this symptom is a nasty one as well. This one, like pain, is the hardest when you are trying to work. You fight all day just to stay awake. You feel sluggish and just wish you could go back to bed. When I work on spreadsheets at work, the fatigue makes it hard not to nod off. Not certain if fatigue is caused by the disease or is a side effect of the medication. Nearly all of the medications that I am on lists fatigue as a symptom, so no wonder I feel like I can barely function.

- *Tremors*—the tremors. I wish there was a machine out there that could mimic what it is like to have tremors. Tremors, stiffness, slurred speech, and the masked facial expression are what cause us, with the disease, the most embarrassment. When I get extremely stressed and the medicine isn't working as it is supposed to, my tremors go into overdrive.

What I mean by this is that my tremors are not only visible on the outside—I get them internally as well. Just imagine your body as being one huge vibrator that you can't shut off. It is horrible. When this happens, I get extreme anxiety, and my head will begin feeling like I have got snakes crawling around inside my brain, and I am petrified of snakes. This can set off a full-blown panic attack.

The tremors are what cause me not to want to go out in public, especially at night. Right now, I am taking my last dose of Sinemet at 5:30 p.m. I normally take a dose during daytime, every three hours, to control the symptoms. By the time 9:00 p.m. rolls around, I don't have enough Sinemet in my system. I try to avoid taking any Sinemet close to bedtime as it can cause nightmares. Plus, the neurologist only prescribes enough to get you to your normal bedtime; meaning, he/she doesn't account for weekends when you might go out to do something. There isn't any magic potion to get you through a long night on a weekend. Because of this, I avoid going out or getting extra anxiety, worrying about whether or not I will shake or lose my balance and fall.

- *Loss of balance*—I have had several incidents where I have fallen. One time, I took such a nasty fall and hit my head that I had trouble walking for nearly eight months. I had to go to physical therapy, and the pain from the exercises would bring me to tears. I really didn't think I would ever be able to walk normally again. Thank goodness I did in time. But because of my tendency to fall, I am scared to walk in the rain, snow, or even on wet grass. I am also scared when I stand up after sitting for quite a while—sometimes, it takes me a few minutes before I can get moving. I also hate going to places where there are events held in grassy areas. I often find that there are small holes that people with no issues can step in and may trip and not fall. If I step into this same hole, I would fall flat on my face. When I walk long distances, my feet would feel like they have bricks tied to the bottom soles of my tennis shoes. This is when I may start dragging a foot or trip a lot. This makes me want to avoid events with a lot of walking. If it is difficult to walk, how am I supposed to exercise?

- *Dressing myself*—so far, this has been a nonissue. I am able to dress myself, put on makeup when I wear it, and fix my hair. My hands do tire easily though, and I have to take breaks when I straighten my hair. I am lucky my tremors are not severe in the morning, so I can function relatively normally.

- *Buying*—I learned the hard way to remove all credit card information from online shopping, which you should do anyway. Once, I didn't realize my card information was saved online at Walmart, and I went to the checkout to see how much shipping would be on an item I was considering, and my shaking caused me to hit the purchase button. Had my stuff not been saved, it wouldn't have mattered, but nope, my luck. I forgot to remove it after my last purchase, so I ended up buying a $250 item that I wasn't planning on buying.

- *Cognitive issues*—Currently, I do experience issues remembering things. If I was to rate this symptom from one to ten, with ten being the worst, I would rate it a four. This one requires me to make notes, just in case, but it rarely interferes with my work or ability to function normally. I could even chalk this symptom up as age-related if I didn't have a diagnosis yet.

- *Masked face*—this one isn't noticeable to many, especially if they didn't know to look for it. I do often get told that I am too serious and need to smile more. This is not as easy as it once was. I have even been told that, maybe, I should drink alcohol more, that it might loosen me up. Clearly, these people need to be educated on Parkinson's.

- *Handwriting*—it is tough to write now. My handwriting is so small and messy that I can barely read what I put down on paper. My hands also start to cramp up if I write quite a bit. So I type everything I can. If not, no one will be able to read what I have down. Good thing I am not a pharmacist or a doctor because I wouldn't be a very effective one if I had to jot things down instead of typing them.

- *Restless legs*—ugh, this one is what will keep me up at night. When I am trying to lay still, my legs have something else in mind. They constantly want to move, and, man, do they ache like crazy.

- *Loss of smell*—I can still smell things, but my ability to smell is not as great as my husband's or daughter's or that of others.

- *Bowel and bladder issues*—this problem is a thorn in my butt. I constantly have constipation, which causes hemorrhoids. I have to take stool softeners often. When I finally get to go, the opposite happens, and I can't stay out of the bathroom. My bladder is one of my biggest issues, preventing me from wanting to go out. Because I no longer have a uterus, cervix, gallbladder, and only one ovary, there isn't much left to hold my bladder into place. Coupled with this, being a known symptom of the disease, I have a double whammy. I have to use the bathroom often, and I am restricted on what events I can go to because I need to sit or be close to a bathroom. I always have to know the bathroom locations before I decide to go anywhere. My self-esteem, because of this, is at an all-time low. I am only fifty-one; I shouldn't have had to be concerned with this issue so early.

Well, I have listed a majority of my Parkinson's symptoms. I am sure there are a few that I missed. There are so many, and it varies day to day and week to week. Once, I compared Parkinson's symptoms with that of multiple sclerosis and found that both diseases are very similar. Not everyone with Parkinson's will experience the same symptoms as me. Their symptoms may be lesser or greater, and as the disease progresses, more symptoms pop up or current ones get worse. There are side effects the longer you are on medication as well.

If you are newly diagnosed, my advice would be not to do too much research in the beginning. I did, and it freaked me out. My anxiety went on high alert. Take it slow and easy. Learn what will manage your symptoms and if that medication will be right for you. Your neurologist may try to talk you into DBS, which is brain surgery, depending on how you react to the medication and how much of it you need and how long you can go between doses. I personally am not considering DBS at this time. I am considering focused ultrasound once the clinical trials end, and it is available everywhere. That is assuming insurance will pay for it. But who knows, with advancements in medications, that I may do a clinical trial? Right now, I am taking it one day at a time, just like many others with chronic diseases. To those battling this disease with me, I will pray for each of us—that a cure is found or at least more medication advancements to help us manage the symptoms with few side effects.

The biggest hurdle many of us with Parkinson's have is that even if there is a new medication to help manage our disease—medication to slow the progression or even cure—many of us won't have access to it. The reason is almost all health insurance carriers don't cover new medications. Even with access to new medications, they don't come out in generic form for years, so a majority of us with Parkinson's won't be able to afford them. For example, monthly, for just these medications, I must pay $409 for my hormone medication, $320 for eye drops for dry eyes, and for my rosacea, nearly $116, and that is for generic. Can you see why many people like myself don't take the medication as prescribed or simply none at all?

# CHAPTER 13

## Dawn's Hope Foundation

Dawn's Hope Inc. was founded April 2022. I established this foundation because on a daily basis, I was hearing from people how they were struggling to find and pay for affordable health coverage. I could relate because I was also struggling to get medication approved by the insurance company, and I had to meet a $3,500 out of pocket deductible every year. My medical expenses were putting me in debt.

For the last seven years, I have worked as a Cobra account manager. I receive calls from people who have lost their health coverage due to a Cobra qualifying event. With no job and very little savings, many of these individuals could not afford the cost of the Cobra coverage.

I knew that someday I would face the same reality. How was I going to be able to pay my insurance and meet the huge deductible once I could no longer work?

The Federal and State Insurance Market place provided affordable monthly insurance premiums. The catch to this program is that the deductibles run in upward of $6,000 or more. While this may be fine for healthier individuals who rarely use the insurance, but for those with chronic health conditions like mine, the annual deductible alone would put me in bankruptcy within a year.

I just had to do something, and something I did was set up this foundation.

At Dawn's Hope Inc., our mission is to ensure that low and middle income individuals and families in the US get the financial assistance they need to help cover the costs of their monthly medical premiums, annual deductibles, and prescriptions.

Our vision is to make sure that everyone has access to health coverage regardless of their ability to pay.

Motto: Have faith, stay hopeful, keep fighting, and never give up!

Dawn's Hope Inc. is a nonprofit corporation, and our 501(c)(e) is pending IRS approval. No employee or board member is being paid. We are 100 percent committed to this cause.

For more information on our foundation, please go to https://dawnshopecharity.org, or you can email us at info@dawnshopecharity.org.

# In Conclusion

I want to thank everyone who took the time to read my story. I hope that if you or someone that you know and care for is fighting a disease, don't lose hope. Anyone who has been abused in any way, what I hope that you get from my story is that don't stay silent, get help, find a way to help others like yourself. Turn something negative into something positive. Be the person that is there for someone in need, even if you can only be there to just listen. You don't have to let your past define you. Don't let your abuser win; if you do, they have victimized you twice. When the self-doubt and negative thoughts creep in to take hold of your soul, think of the verses in the following songs:

- Lee Brice's song "Lies":

  Yeah, the cruelest lies of all the lies we tell
  Are the ones we tell ourselves

  But [you] ain't ready to quit

  Yeah, it's okay to struggle, okay to be scared
  Yeah, the busted and broken can be repaired

- Mandisa's song "Overcomer":

  Stay in the fight until the final round
  You're not going under,
  'Cause God is holding you right now

- Katy Nicole's song "In Jesus Name":

  I pray for your healing
  That circumstances will change
  I pray that the fear inside you would flee in Jesus name
  I pray miracles over your life in Jesus name

Keep the faith. We can do this! Sending my love and prayers your way!

# Important Sites and Hotline

If you want to see if sex offenders are living next to you, you can do a search here: *https://www.familywatchdog.us/default.asp*

If you want to do a search to see if a specific person has any child abuse charges, you can go to *publicsrecords.com*

National Suicide Prevention Lifeline: 1-800-273-8255.

# References

https://www.apa.org
https://www.arkofhopeforchildren.org
https://www.childwelfare.gov
https://www.d2l.org
https://www.focusonthefamily.com/pro-life/child-abuse-what-should-we-know/
https://www.healthyandnaturalworld.com
https://www.history.com/topics/vietnam-war/agent-orange-1
https://www.hopkinsmedicine.org
https://www.mayoclinic.org
https://www.mayoclinic.org/diseases-conditions/child-abuse/symptoms-causes/syc-20370864
https://www.michaeljfox.org
https://www.ncbi.nlm.nih.gov
https://www.parkinson.org
https://www.psychiatry.org
https://www.rainn.org/articles/child-sexual-abuse
https://www.verywellhealth.com
https://www.webmd.com

# Songs

- "Overcomer" by Mandisa
- "You're Gonna Be Okay" by Jenn Johnson
- "Fear Is a Liar" by Zach Williams
- "Survivor" by Zach Williams
- "Rise Up" by Andra Day
- "Just Be Held" by Casting Crowns
- "Lies" by Lee Brice
- "In Jesus' Name" by Katy Nichole

# About the Author

Dawn Howard, a native of Missouri, currently resides in Columbia, Missouri, home to the University of Missouri and one of the fourth most populated cities in Missouri. She lives with her ex-husband and her two dogs, Dakota and Aadya.

Besides writing her first book, detailing her life as an abused child, who is now living with Parkinson's, she has established a charitable foundation called *Dawn's Hope Inc.* It is her mission to help people who are dealing with incurable chronic diseases and the financial struggles of having access to affordable new medications and treatments not covered by health insurance

www.ingramcontent.com/pod-product-compliance
Lightning Source LLC
Chambersburg PA
CBHW031409160726
47993CB00003B/1153

*9798886441697*